where inspiration lives

where inspiration lives

WRITERS, ARTISTS, AND THEIR CREATIVE PLACES

EDITED BY JOHN MILLER AND AARON KENEDI

NEW WORLD LIBRARY
NOVATO, CALIFORNIA

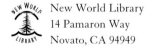 New World Library
14 Pamaron Way
Novato, CA 94949

Cover and interior design: Miller Media
New World Library editor: Jason Gardner
Production: Mary Ann Casler
Cover photograph: Joel Meyerowitz
Copyediting and proofreading: Mimi Kusch and Annelise Zamula

Library of Congress Cataloging-in-Publication Data
Where inspiration lives : writers, artists, and their creative places /
edited by John Miller and Aaron Kenedi
    p.   cm.
ISBN 1-57731-241-4
1. Authors, American—Homes and haunts—United States. 2. Artists—
Homes and haunts—United States. 3. Creation (Literary, artistic, etc.).
4. Place (Philosophy) in literature. I. Miller, John. II. Kenedi, Aaron.
PS141.W48 2003
810.9—dc21   2002035971

First printing, April 2003
ISBN 1-57731-241-4
Printed in Hong Kong
Distributed to the trade by Publishers Group West

10 9 8 7 6 5 4 3 2 1

SPECIAL THANKS TO
AMY RENNERT
AND JASON GARDNER

contents

introduction

JOHN MILLER AND AARON KENEDI

IN 1929, GEORGIA O'KEEFFE took a short vacation to Abiquiu, New Mexico. She would never be the same.

"If you ever go to New Mexico," she wrote, "it will change your life."

Soon the desert was in O'Keeffe's blood. Desperate, she hauled cow skulls and bones back east, trying to take the country and its inspiration with her. (Unfortunately, friends kind enough to drive her eventually objected to their trunks being stuffed with bones.)

In 1949, O'Keeffe moved permanently to Abiquiu, where she would create some of the most enduring images of the American West.

Place transformed O'Keeffe, as it has

many writers and artists. Who can think of Hemingway without envisioning Spanish bullfights or the blue waters of the Caribbean? William Faulkner is inseparable from his imagined Yoknapatawpha County. And the diverse art of Martin Scorsese, Dorothy Parker, and Spike Lee is infused with the New York they inhabit.

Where Inspiration Lives looks at how ten writers and artists have been affected by their home surroundings. Some are hip and irreverent, some traditional; some are urban, some rural; some adopted their place, others were born there. But they've all experienced landscapes, homes, or workplaces that have inspired luminous creativity.

Eudora Welty, who spent her entire life in the Jackson, Mississippi, home that her father built, is a perfect example of creative spirit being intertwined with place. Her deeply original novels and autobiography paint amazingly vivid pictures of her home.

To Welty, writing and place were inseparable. Her essay "Place in Fiction" bemoans the demotion of place in much modern writing.

"All fiction is bound up in place," she said. "It is through place that we put out roots, wherever birth, chance, fate or our traveling selves set us down; but where those roots reach toward is the deep and running vein, eternal and consistent and everywhere purely itself, that feeds and is fed by the human understanding."

But you don't have to live in your hometown your whole life to feel the deep pull of place. Many writers and painters travel far and wide, but are always moved by one spot. Texas-born Larry McMurtry lived in the East for much of his life before returning to his hometown of Archer City. While McMurtry wrote his best-selling novels elsewhere, it is to this town—the setting for *The Last Picture Show*—that he has come to build his ultimate dream: a community bookstore.

It's the same with far-flung travel writer Peter Matthiessen. He's documented the four corners of the earth, but has always returned to Long Island, his refuge.

Creativity strikes in very personal ways. A place that is inspiring to one may be stifling to another. Terry McMillan's East Bay hills are the perfect setting for her writing, but for very different reasons than one might think. Thirty-five years earlier, the painter Richard Diebenkorn left those same hills and, against the grave advice of friends, moved to a beach town just north of Los Angeles. It was there, in a light-filled loft, that he blossomed, creating signature works of the hazy Southern California landscape.

Anne Rice's overgrown New Orleans lair couldn't be any more different than the spartan California Zen abode of Gary Snyder. But as disparate as they are, they work the same inspirational magic for each writer.

Henry David Thoreau may claim the

most famous experience of the transformative powers of place. From 1845 to 1847, the author lived in a small, rustic cabin on the shores of Walden Pond, outside Concord, Massachusetts. There, he was inspired to examine his life and man's relationship with the land. Out of this examination came his seminal work, *Walden, or Life in the Woods.* Thoreau admitted he could have never created this work had he not visited Walden Pond:

> *I cannot come nearer to God and Heaven*
> *Than I live to Walden even.*
> *I am its stony shore,*
> *And the breeze that passes o'er;*
> *In the hollow of my hand*
> *Are its water and its sand,*
> *And its deepest resort*
> *Lies high in my thought.*

where inspiration lives

sagaponack

PETER MATTHIESSEN

PETER MATTHIESSEN has built an
extraordinary reputation writing about far-
away lands and exotic cultures. His novels and
essays are rich with the visceral tales of
African tribesmen, Nepalese wildlife, and
Siberian ecology. At the least, he is, as some
have called him, the hardest-working travel
writer in the world.

But after nearly fifty years of writing about
places abroad, Matthiessen began to turn his
attention homeward—to the shores of Long
Island, New York, and his own personal writing environment.

Sitting in his studio, he says: "You could

PETER MATTHIESSEN IN HIS STUDIO. PHOTO BY ARNOLD NEWMAN.

write a whole story of my life just looking around this room."

As *Esquire* magazine reported in 1989, "The room is actually a converted playhouse across the grass from the writer's home. Every vertical space that isn't an overfilled bookcase or an odd-shaped window looking out onto the flat coastal land is covered to the reach of a tall man's arm with clippings, scribbled quotes, pictures, maps, postcards, addresses, feathers. Every horizontal space with the exception of his long, built-in desk and rickety office chair, is a museum."

His 1986 book *Men's Lives* is a moving tribute to the three-hundred-year-old culture of the commercial fishermen of the South Fork of Long Island. After twenty-five years away, Matthiessen was drawn back to the place he worked as a young man. In his preface the author lovingly describes the landscape that has served as refuge throughout his career:

"Two humpback whales, the first I have

"I like to hear and smell the countryside, the land my characters inhabit."

seen in a decade, roll softly on the surface, like black shining rocks in the silver ocean. . . . They move slowly to the east, off the narrow strip of sand that separates Georgica Pond from the Atlantic. . . .

"I walked down to the ocean for a breath of air. The day was cold, with a northwest wind shivering the rainwater where ice was broken in the puddles. Rising and falling in flight along the dunes, a flock of gulls picked up the last ambient light from the red embers in the west. The silent birds, undulating on the wind, shone bone white against massed somber grays, low over the ocean; the cloud bank looked ominous, like waiting winter.

"From the beach landing, in this moody sky and twilight, I saw something awash in the white foam, perhaps a quarter mile down to the eastward. The low heavy thing, curved round upon itself, did not look like driftwood; I thought at first that it must be a human body. Uneasy, I walked east a little way, then

"In any writing you're paying attention to detail . . . good writing is administering a series of tiny astonishments."

A BEACHED SPERM WHALE ON LONG ISLAND. PHOTO BY DOUG KUNTZ.

LONG ISLAND FISHERMEN. PHOTO BY DOUG KUNTZ.

hurried ahead; the thing was not driftwood, not a body, but the great clean skull of a finback whale, dark bronze with sea water and minerals. The beautiful form, crouched like some ancient armored creature in the wash, seemed to await me. No one else was on the beach, which was clean of tracks. There was only the last cold fire of dusk, the white birds fleeing toward the darkness, the frosty foam whirling around the skull, seeking to regather it into the deeps.

"By the time I returned with a truck and chain, it was nearly night. The sea was higher, and the skull was settling like some enormous crab into the wash; I could not get close enough without sinking the truck down to the axles. I took careful bearings on the skull's location, and a good thing, too, because four hours later, when the tide had turned, the massive skull had sunk away into the sands, all but what looked like a small dark rock in the moon-white shallows. I dug this out

"I walked down to the ocean for a breath of air. The day was cold, with a northwest wind shivering the rainwater where ice was broken in the puddles."

"Often I go
out alone, for
walking in
solitude
through the
dim glades,
immersed in
silence, one
learns a lot
that cannot be
learned in any
other way."

enough to secure a hawser, then ran this rope above the tide line, as a lead to the skull's location the next morning. But fearing that an onshore wind or storm might bury it forever, I went down at dead low tide that night, under the moon, and dug the skull clear and worked it up out of its pit, using truck and chain. Nearly six feet across, the skull was waterlogged and heavy, five hundred pounds or better. Not until one in the morning— spending more time digging out my truck than freeing the bone—did I hitch it high enough onto the beach to feel confident that the tide already coming in would not rebury it. By morning there was onshore wind, with a chop already making up from the southwest, but the whale skull was still waiting at the water's edge. Bud Topping came down with his tractor and we took it home. When Milt Miller, who was raised by the old whalers, had a look at it a few weeks later, he said it was the biggest skull he ever saw."

Matthiessen, whose characters are often victims and refugees in a material world, has spent nearly seventy-five years accumulating the things that please him and adjusting his surroundings.

For the last forty of those years, he has risen early and come to this place to work, usually taking an afternoon break to cut wood or play touch football. Much of his book *On the River Styx, and Other Stories* was done here.

"I hate to travel now," he told *Esquire*. "I get homesick halfway to New York." It's an odd comment coming from a man who has written of the world's farthermost places. But somehow it begins to make sense. There is an equilibrium here between man and place that is somehow perfectly evolved. This place is Peter Matthiessen's natural habitat.

"I don't want these characters to step off the page, I want them to step out of the landscape."

abiquiu

GEORGIA O'KEEFFE

PERHAPS NO PAINTER is more asso-
ciated with a landscape than Georgia
O'Keeffe. In 1929, the artist was hiking
through rugged hills north of Abiquiu, New
Mexico, when she discovered an abandoned
ranch. These broken-down buildings, known
as Ghost Ranch, would soon become her
home—and her inspiration. Biographer
Jeffrey Hogrefe describes an old friend visiting
her ranch:

"In the summer of 1951, Georgia O'Keeffe
fetched Anita Pollitzer, from the airport in
Santa Fe. The night after she arrived, Anita
was sleeping soundly when, at four-thirty in

AT JUAN HAMILTON'S ABIQUIU STUDIO. PHOTO BY TODD WEBB.

THE ABIQUIU STUDIO. PHOTO BY TODD WEBB.

the morning, she heard a knock at the door. O'Keeffe was standing before her in a white kimono and Mexican sandals.

"'Come quickly,' she implored her tired guest, 'You mustn't miss the dawn. It will never be just like this again.'

"O'Keeffe led her blurry-eyed friend through the interior of the adobe house and into a patio where jimsonweeds bloomed in the cold, dark air. They entered an adobe garden overlooking the Chama River and the land formations of Abiquiu. They stared in awe at the spectacular light show that had inspired O'Keeffe more than thirty years earlier and would continue to inspire her for thirty more."

The ranch, which the artist painstakingly rebuilt, featured an enormous one-acre garden of exotic poppies, bamboo, red raspberries, cactus, and lime and peach trees. Her studio overlooked the deep crimson mountains that became the subject of many of her greatest works. When the artist wasn't

"When I first came to New Mexico, I was so crazy about it, I thought, how can I take part of it with me to work on?"

here, she was at the studio of her protégé, Juan Hamilton. Hamilton's studio also captured the magic of Abiquiu: "It has a very white feeling," O'Keeffe wrote. "The desert light comes in through the skylights, beautiful light. It makes the room seem very alive."

More than anything, O'Keeffe's letters most passionately describe what made Abiquiu such a source of inspiration:

[To Anita Pollitzer, 1916]

TONIGHT I WALKED into the sunset to mail some letters and the whole sky—there is so much of it here—was just blazing and grey blue clouds were rioting all through the hotness of it . . . I walked out past the last house, past the locust tree and sat on the fence for a long time, looking, just looking into the lightning. You see there was nothing but sky . . . there was a wonderful moon. . . .

It is absurd the way I love this country.

"The bones seem to cut sharply to the center of something that is keenly alive in the desert…"

GEORGIA O'KEEFFE, *WALL WITH GREEN DOOR.*

... And the sky, Anita, you have never seen such sky. It is wonderful.

[To Anita Pollitzer, 1948]

WHEN I FIRST CAME to New Mexico in the summer of 1929, I was so crazy about it, I thought, how can I take part of it with me to work on? There was nothing to see in the land in the way of flowers. There were just dry white bones. So I picked them up. I took a barrel of bones back to New York. They were symbols of my desert. To me they are as beautiful as anything I know. The bones seem to cut sharply to the center of something that is keenly alive in the desert, even though it is vast and empty and untouchable—and knows no kindness with all its beauty.

[To William Schubart, 1950]

I CAN NOT TELL you how pleased I am to be back in this world again. The brightest

"I have slept out under the stars. There isn't a crack of the waking day or night that isn't full."

yellow is gone from the long line of cottonwood trees and the wide flat stretch in front of them, all warm with autumn grass, and the unchanging mountain behind the valley, they all moved right into my room to me. I was amused.

It is a beautiful world here . . . it is very good to be back. I feel strange about the bones that I leave in New York, that I have left them all shut up in an odd pen they can't get out of.

As I sit here writing, seated on a large cushion at the foot of the bed, using a stool for a table, I see the large almost full pale gold moon rise up out of the horizon at the end of the mountain. Needless to say, that is why I am writing here instead of a desk. The moon came up with such a soft feeling, then as the sky darkens over the moon it becomes brighter, more brilliant.

[To William Schubart, 1950]
I wish you were here tonight. The night is fine, the moon is so bright. The

"Tonight I walked into the sunset . . . and the whole sky . . . was just blazing and grey blue clouds were rioting all through the hotness of it."

"It is absurd
the way I love
this country."

POURING TEA AT THE GHOST RANCH HOUSE. PHOTO BY TODD WEBB.

patio walls are warm and alive in the cool bright moonlight. One very bright star is over the southwest corner of the patio. . . . The walls are the walls of the rooms with a few openings into the patio; and they are the soft warm adobe that one always wants to touch, or sometimes feels it is too fine to touch, one should just leave it there alone, remote, untouched. . . .

I haven't written in a long time, I know. I've been doing odd things. You know there are Indians out here who sing and dance to make the corn grow, to bless the home, to cure the sick. I've gone to two all night dances: one in a village about 250 miles away—the Shallico—at Zuni, the blessing of the home. The other about the same distance, in another direction, up a very rough mountain road newly built or cut for the occasion. It's a Navajo ceremony that has to do with curing the sick and also with a kind of adoration of fire that I don't understand, but I would say more than 1,200 people gathered out there in the night, built big fires, particularly a big central fire, surrounded by some fifteen smaller fires with an enclosure of pine boughs. Teams of twenty or thirty came in and danced and sang all night. They all bring food and eat around the fires, evening and morning. The singing and dancing amid the green and the smoke, the fire, and stars. It is quite wonderful. . . .

LADDER AND ADOBE WALL, ABIQUIU.
PHOTO BY TODD WEBB.

archer city

LARRY MCMURTRY

FORTY YEARS AGO, Larry McMurtry left Archer City. The Texas-born author gained great fame—and a Pulitzer Prize—for his novels *Lonesome Dove, Terms of Endearment, The Last Picture Show,* and *Texasville.* Much of his writing debunked the romantic West of Hollywood, painting a portrait of a ruthless, lonely country.

But this is the country that's in McMurtry's blood. In 1991, while living on the East Coast, he suffered a heart attack and then a bout with depression. He packed up and returned home to the family ranch where he grew up, near Archer City, the small town that was the

MCMURTRY IN HIS BOOKSTORE. PHOTO BY MICHAEL O'BRIEN.

model for Thalia in *The Last Picture Show* and *Texasville*.

"I never had a sense of being away from home. I visited Archer City often," McMurtry explains. His ties to Archer City run deep; his grandfather originally came here in the 1880s.

"I live in my grandparents' house," McMurtry says. "I have a large family—all cowboys first and last."

"It's still such a strong landscape for me. . . . I spent a lot of time in New York, Washington, and L.A., and a fair amount of time in Europe. I took the measure of several powerful places. But it just got to be where the homing instinct came over me, and I wanted to be in Texas a little bit more. It's kind of a normal pattern—you go out into the world and then bring what you want of the world back home with you."

Archer City lies in the middle of North Texas's rolling plain country. The film version of *The Last Picture Show* was shot in

"[Archer City is] a strong landscape for me . . . you go out into the world and then bring what you want of the world back home with you."

THE LAST PICTURE SHOW WAS SET IN THALIA, BASED ON ARCHER CITY.

Archer City and depicts a dusty, one-stoplight town. And it hasn't changed much.

But Larry McMurtry did not move back to Texas to retire. Instead, he brought two hundred thousand books with him and opened Booked Up, a used and antiquarian bookstore, the largest business in Archer City.

"I think of my bookshop as a book ranch—a large one," says McMurtry. While it draws visitors from around the country, the store is also a center for Archer City's book lovers, a tight-knit, laid-back community. A sign in Booked Up reads:

"If you are unable to locate an employee in this building, please feel free to wander about yelling yoo hoo and peering into the storage rooms until completely frustrated. Then proceed to Building One where you will find patronizing employees busy at work or sitting around drinking coffee and laughing at you."

When you see Larry McMurtry among the

"I live in my grandparents' house. I have a large family— all cowboys first and last."

shelves, it is clear that he is at home. Writer Mark Horowitz describes the day he found the author in his element:

"There he is, working in the huge back room of the main building, surrounded by towering white bookshelves holding tens of thousands of books. More arrive every month, and as McMurtry talks, he never stops working his way through a new shipment of contemporary fiction, bought from a collector in Virginia. He flips open every book, scans the title page and pencils a price inside the front cover. . . . As a bookplate he uses a tiny strip of paper marked with the McMurtry brand, the same one his father and grandfather used to mark their cattle.

"'I want to have the biggest bookstore I can, and still have good books,' McMurtry says. 'I like expensive ones, but I also like humbler books that people can read.'"

Right now, Booked Up has more than one hundred thousand volumes. Young

"I think of my bookshop as a book ranch— a large one."

COTTON AND REPLANTED GRASSLAND ON TEXAS PLAINS. PHOTO BY TOM BEAN.

employees move like worker ants between the four buildings, wheeling handcarts loaded with new arrivals. The main building—a former car dealership—holds rare books, biographies, belles-lettres, and Western Americana. Across the street, history, poetry, and twentieth-century English and American fiction are housed, while down the block a separate building is devoted to nineteenth-century books, literature in translation, and books about books. (An annex opposite the courthouse handles drama, music, dance, and film.)

The staff is small, and some buildings are often left unlocked and unattended, but McMurtry is unconcerned. "'I don't think we have many book thieves here in Archer City,'" he says, smiling.

After returning home and remodeling a big old house, he's bent on remaking Archer City into a place with books and theaters and restaurants and a steady stream of visitors

"...It just got to be where the homing instinct came over me, and I wanted to be in Texas a little bit more."

from all over the world—the Archer City of his dreams. If it works, it will be *The Last Picture Show* with a happy ending, a strange and touching and unexpected reconciliation. Whatever happens, this is the closing of another chapter for McMurtry, and the start of a new one. He is rewriting his hometown.

When you see McMurtry among the bookshelves, it is clear that he is at home.

new orleans

ANNE RICE

ANNE RICE, BEST-SELLING AUTHOR
of *The Vampire Chronicles* and other fictional
excursions into the bizarre and fantastic, likes
to give tours of her large, antebellum mansion
in New Orleans. "There's the fireplace where
Rowan and Lasher sat on Christmas morning,"
she says matter of-factly, a smile tugging at
her lips.

A witch and her evil spiritual companion,
Rowan and Lasher are characters in Rice's
novel *The Witching Hour*, set largely in the
house. . . . The room, furnished exactly as it is
in the book, is calm, immaculate. No blood
stains the beautiful Oriental carpet, no gore

ANNE RICE AND FAMILY AT HOME IN NEW ORLEANS. PHOTO BY RICK OLIVIER.

clings to the silk curtains or the tasseled sofa.

Up a flight of stairs, to Rice's office, where she ignores the messy desk and points dramatically to an ornate bed—"where Dierdre died," she says, of another of the book's characters.

Up another flight, to her husband's studio. "This is where Stuart Townsend's body lay, you know," she says, gazing at the floor, her voice pensive. . . .

What is unnerving about all this is not that Rice switches back and forth between her fictional and factual worlds, but that they seem to coexist with equal intensity. It is as if she has somehow brought about the haunting of her own house.

"Well, I think that's true," she says thoughtfully. "If a ghost is a projection of a strong environment, then I imagine the characters could take on some kind of life…."

One of four sisters, Anne grew up on the edge of—not in—the old moneyed Garden

"I write to be read, to create something that other people will read, care about, and enjoy."

District of New Orleans. She wandered the neighborhoods, imagining how people lived in the big houses. In the seventh grade, she wrote a "novel"—"well, I filled a whole note-book"—about aliens who come to earth and eventually commit suicide.

Her father worked for the post office and wrote fiction (unpublished) in the evenings. Her mother, Katherine, combined Southern-belle charm with strict Catholicism. "She'd get us up for Mass," Rice recalls. "She'd say, 'The body and blood of Christ is on that altar, now get out of that bed!'" Katherine warned her daughters never to "let a boy kiss you until the ring is on your finger," but had a tol-erant view of sex itself. She told wonderful stories, and Anne loved her.

Katherine was also an alcoholic who drank not for pleasure but to pass out. Rice refuses to edit the horror: "I remember thinking, 'What I would give, for just one day, to feel like everybody else.'"

"[My books] are meant to be in those backpacks on the Berkeley campus, along with Castaneda and Tolstoy and anybody else."

ST. LOUIS CATHEDRAL, NEW ORLEANS. PHOTO BY MIKE BRINSON.

When Rice was fifteen, her mother died. "It was from alcoholism," Rice says, her mouth tight. "As a matter of fact, I think she swallowed her tongue. . . ."

Rice left the Catholic church three years after her mother's death. "My faith just went," she says. "It struck me as really evil—the idea you could go to hell for French-kissing someone. . . . I didn't believe Jesus Christ was the Son. I didn't believe one had to be Catholic in order to go to heaven. I didn't believe heaven existed, either."

But Catholic rites, and doomed mothers, became frequent themes. The passage in which Lestat saves his mother, one of the most moving and shocking in Rice's work, is in a section called "Viaticum for the Marquise." The viaticum is the last communion given to a person at the point of death; in this case, it was Lestat's vampire blood, which he offers his mother after draining her of mortal blood.

In a sense, Rice is returning the vampires to

"I think the imagination is bisexual. Once you're 'out of nature' . . . you see all people as beautiful. . . ."

their former splendor. . . . Rice turns vampire conventions inside out. Her immortals enjoy looking at themselves in mirrors, do not flinch before crucifixes, and ignore garlic. They avoid the dank decay of the grave and slurp their bloody draughts in splendor; they wear fine clothes and enjoy fine art. Impotent, they are somehow also bisexual. "Well, I think the imagination is bisexual," Rice says. "Once you're 'out of nature,' to use Yeats's phrase, you see all people as beautiful and you make a bond to people of your own sex as easily as to people of the opposite sex. . . ."

"I think what's important is that you write what's really, really intense, and what gives you the greatest thrill," Rice says. "All I know is that the supernatural gives me that intensity whether I'm reading it or writing it. I just find it the most powerful means that I have for writing about real life."

She means it literally: the passionate energy that infuses Rice's prose is personal. *Interview*

"I think what's important is that you write what's really, really intense, and what gives you the greatest thrill."

THE ARTIST IN HER HOME. PHOTO BY RICK OLIVIER.

with the Vampire, the darkest of her stories, is also the most painful in its autobiographical material. In 1972, when she and her husband, Stan, were living in Berkeley, California, their five-year-old daughter, Michelle, died of leukemia.

"It was a nightmare," Rice remembers. . . . After Michelle's death, she and Stan began drinking heavily. She took a job to distract herself, but it didn't work. At Stan's urging, she turned to writing full time. She had nothing to lose, she says: "I was nothing and nobody. I had no prestige. I wasn't a mother. I was a bad wife—I never cleaned house. I was no good at anything."

Writing at night in a corner of the bedroom while her husband slept, Rice went back to an earlier story she had written, about an eighteenth-century vampire in New Orleans. Unaware, she says, of the significance of what she was doing, she added a beautiful little girl with golden curls (like Michelle), whom the

"I find [the supernatural] the most powerful means that I have for writing about real life."

vampires save from mortal death by making her a vampire.

"Suddenly, when I was in the skin of Louis, when I was in this cartoon character . . . when I slipped into this seemingly unreal thing and looked through his eyes, I could make my whole world real," she says. "He was able to say, 'Let me tell you about New Orleans, this was our world,' and I could write about all the beauty. Even the most fictional stuff in there was somehow out of my real world. It fell into place and was coherent." . . .

In sharp contrast to the sadness of those years, Rice's life today is one of domestic tranquility. She and Stan Rice met in a high-school journalism class in Texas. "I fell for him right away," she says. "I just never fell out of love." They got married in 1961, when she was twenty, and went together to San Francisco State College, where Rice studied political science. Later, after a stint at graduate school studying literary

"I was nothing and nobody. I had no prestige. I wasn't a mother. I was a bad wife— I never cleaned house. I was no good at anything."

criticism, she got a master's degree in creative writing.

The couple have a twelve-year-old son, Christopher, born six years after Michelle's death. Rice stopped drinking during her pregnancy, and she and Stan quit altogether in 1979—"for Chris's sake." Tall and blond, Stan was the inspiration for Lestat—"the good parts," his wife adds hastily. . . .

In 1988, the family moved to New Orleans, after twenty-seven years in San Francisco. The house, bought with her advance for *The Witching Hour*, is filled with good furniture, Stan's "post-Primitive" paintings, African artifacts they've collected, and Rice's collection of dolls. Rice is ecstatic about the move: the city feels right to her, the sunsets and the flowers are all that she remembered. People greet her warmly in shops and restaurants. . . .

"I'm picking up threads here that were totally ruptured by leaving," Rice says. "I feel complete, at peace, less afraid of dying."

"I'll never really be an insider. I've been accepted with all my madness...but I'm still not a Garden District woman."

Somehow, her thrill-bent imagination fits into this quiet life. . . .

For years a semi-recluse in San Francisco… Rice has begun since coming back to New Orleans to shape a more social life for herself—family reunions, opening her house to a historical-society tour, and giving dinner parties. But this has risks. Can a writer whose most moving work has been about outsiders, who has drawn heavily from her own pain and a restless search for self, achieve the literary acclaim she so desperately wants now that she is, for all practical purposes, a happy insider?

"I'll never really be an insider," Rice says fiercely, as if surprised that anyone might think so. "I've been accepted with all my madness—they don't throw rocks at the house because of it—but I'm still not a Garden District woman. I see them when I take my walks. They have shoulder-length hair. They are lovely human beings. But we are still basically outsiders who live inside this house."

"Stick with writing no matter what. Believe in yourself. . . . People will try to tear you down. Ignore them. It takes courage."

This article was written by Susan Ferraro and originally appeared in The New York Times Magazine, *October 14, 1990.*

kitkitdizze

GARY SNYDER

ONE HUNDRED AND FIFTY MILES north of San Francisco, through the storied California gold country, the Sierra foothills stretch broadly, joining the cresting mountains to the Sacramento valley basin.

Take a left turn off Highway 20 and onto rustic Highway 49 and you'll find yourself winding along a twisting rivergrade that is breathtaking both for its beauty and its danger.

Push even farther out, past the tiny town of North San Juan and the craggy, desolate remnants of the Malakoff Diggings gold mines and eventually you will come to a place almost laughably remote and infinitely beautiful.

SNYDER IN THE SIERRA FOOTHILLS, NORTHERN CALIFORNIA. PHOTO BY ED KASHI.

"We were
cash poor and
land rich. . . .
We needed to
rethink our
relationship
to this place,
with its
busy—almost
downtown—
rush of plants
and creatures."

For thirty-three years this place teeming with plant and animal life has been Gary Snyder's muse. It's here that Snyder crafts poetry that's symbiotic with the continent he calls Turtle Island. The Pulitzer Prize–winning poet writes of this relationship so often and so passionately, he has moved from being best-known as one of the original Beat poets to being one of our most eloquent spokesmen for ecological preservation worldwide.

While today Snyder's one-hundred-acre retreat displays certain modern conveniences such as telephone access and electric (albeit solar) power, back in 1969 it was practically un-inhabitable. As Snyder wrote in *Audubon* mag-azine, "At that time there were virtually no neighbors . . . no power lines, no phones, and [it was] twenty five miles—across a canyon—to town."

Snyder and his family chose a spot ringed by Douglas firs, tall pines, and sturdy oak trees. They cleared the area of manzanita and other brush and he set up a workspace for himself where he could write. He and his wife named the place "Kitkitdizze" after a sticky, sweet-smelling shrub that was abundant and durable in the foothills; it seemed the perfect symbol of the Snyders's new home.

"We had our hands full for the first ten years just getting up walls and roofs, bathhouse, small barn, washhouse. A lot of it was done the old way: We dropped all the trees to be used in the frame of the house with a two-man falling saw and peeled them with drawknives. Light was from kerosene lamps; we heated with wood and cooked with wood and propane. Wood-burning ranges, wood-burning sauna stoves, treadle-operated sewing machines, and propane-using Servel refrigerators from the fifties were the targets of highly selective shopping runs.

"Many other young settlers found their place in Northern California back in the early

"Living in a place like this is absolutely delicious. Coyote howl fugues, owl exchanges in the treetops, the almost daily sighting of deer. . . ."

"Place is a
relationship
like a marriage.
Either you
enter into that
relationship,
and it's very
rewarding, or
you deny that
relationship,
and you live
in loneliness."

SNYDER AT WORK AT KITKITDIZZE STUDIO. PHOTO BY ED KASHI.

seventies, so eventually there was a whole reinhabitory culture living this way."

Of his rural existence on the North San Juan Ridge, Snyder writes in his 1996 book *A Place in Space*: "My family and I decided from early on to try to be here, in the mid-elevation forests of the Sierra Nevada, as fully as we could. This brave attempt was backed by lack of resources and a lot of dumb bravado. We figured that simplicity would of itself be beautiful, and we had our own extravagant notions of ecological morality. But necessity was the teacher that finally showed us how to live as part of the natural community."

Living a lifetime as part of the natural community, Snyder has developed the twin approaches of the "etiquette of freedom" and the "practice of the wild" as salve for the current global ecological crisis.

"It comes down to how one thinks about screens, fences, or dogs. These are often used for keeping the wild at bay. . . . We came to

"Care for the environment is like *noblesse oblige*. You don't do it because it has to be done. You do it because it's beautiful."

live a permeable, porous life in our house set among the stands of oak and pine. Our buildings are entirely opened up for the long Sierra summer. Mud daubers make their trips back and forth from inside the house to the edge of the pond like tireless little cement trucks, and pour their foundations on beams, in cracks, and (if you're not alert) in rifle-bore holes and backpack fire-pump nozzles. . . . For mosquitoes, which are never much of a problem, the house is just another place to enjoy the shade. At night the bats dash around the rooms, in and out of the open skylights, swoop down past your cheek and go out an open sliding door. In the dark of the night the deer can be heard stretching for the lower leaves of the apple trees, and at dawn the wild turkeys are strolling a few yards from the bed."

Such observations about environment have been at the heart of Snyder's work for more than forty years. From *Turtle Island*, his Pulitzer Prize–winning collection of poems in

"Beyond all this studying and managing, there's another level to knowing nature. . . . Nature often just flits by and is not easily seen in a hard, clear light."

THE SNYDER COMPOUND, NORTH SAN JUAN, CALIFORNIA. PHOTO BY ED KASHI.

1975, to *Rivers and Mountains Without End*, his 1997 opus of fourteen poems, he has maintained a steadfast focus on promoting man and nature symbiosis. *The Los Angeles Times* has even called him "the greatest of living nature poets."

After the two trekked through the Sierra Nevadas together, Beat compatriot Jack Kerouac paid homage to Snyder in his 1958 classic *Dharma Bums* by creating the character Japhy Ryder, a mountain-climbing, Zen poet. Ryder was depicted as a new breed of counter-culture hero: a man who took his Zen practice beyond the confines of formal study and into the everyday.

Despite living a life dedicated to the solitary observation of wilderness, Snyder has managed to be one of the most visible American poets, as well as one of the most steady and prolific. He has taught English literature at the University of California at Davis since 1985 and is a frequent lecturer up and down the West Coast. By

"We may not transform reality, but we may transform ourselves. And if we transform ourselves, we might just change the world a bit."

his own reckoning he has seen "practically every university in the United States."

Embracing the responsibility of the place and the moment is his prescription. Another key principle in this creative stewardship is waking up to "wild mind." He clarifies that "wild" in this context does not mean chaotic, excessive, or crazy.

"It means self-organizing," he says. "It means elegantly self-disciplined, self-regulating, self-maintained. That's what wilderness is. Nobody has to do the management plan for it. So I say to people, 'let's trust in the self-disciplined elegance of wild mind.' Practically speaking, a life that is vowed to simplicity, appropriate boldness, good humor, gratitude, unstinting work and play, and lots of walking, brings us close to the actually existing world and its wholeness."

"Maybe I won't be a writer anymore. Maybe I'll clean out my barn."

ocean park

RICHARD DIEBENKORN

IN 1966, RICHARD DIEBENKORN, by then a successful painter, did something unheard of. He packed his family and moved from intellectual Berkeley to the wasteland of Los Angeles. New York art critics were already suspicious of this painter who eschewed New York to live in the West. But Southern California?

"They all asked, 'Why go to *that place*?'" Diebenkorn recalled. "I first came down here in 1961...and really responded to Los Angeles. Because I had pretty much gone along with my father's judgment about Los Angeles being this big town, and it wasn't a

SANTA MONICA, CALIFORNIA. PHOTO BY RYAN MCVAY.

city at all. There was nothing, no real reason to come down here. But when I came down . . . it seemed like a place to live, and I think that sort of brewed."

Diebenkorn settled in Ocean Park, a small beach town next to Santa Monica. It was here he would spend the next two decades and produce his signature work.

"I loved the pace," explained Diebenkorn, "the attitude, just the things one might pick up in several days of driving around, talking to people—being [with] other artists who were there, and printers, and just sort of catching something of their lives and something of the life of Los Angeles, which seemed, surprisingly, quite attractive.

"I had seen Los Angeles in a new light. And there was considerable vitality artistically, as we know, and the pace was pretty exciting to me. Very different from the North."

Shortly after relocating, Diebenkorn abandoned his widely admired style, evocative of

"I have always been a landscape artist."

his idols Bonnard and Edward Hopper, and created something startlingly new. The new paintings were abstract, but the Southern California landscape—hazy light, flat land, open sea—figured largely. He titled them *Ocean Park*.

"I have always been a landscape artist," explained Diebenkorn. The new canvases could have never been painted in New York; they *exuded* Southern California. And they were great. Even New York critics were won over. The premier critic Robert Hughes described the revolutionary new pieces:

"The *Ocean Park*s are surely one of the most distinguished meditations on landscape in painting since Monet's water lilies. The landscape in question is that of the Pacific coast of Southern California, seen through the large transom windows of Diebenkorn's studio. High air, planes of sea, and lines of road, fence, pier, and window frame, crystalline light, an encompassing blueness. The paintings are

"I had seen Los Angeles in a new light . . . the pace was pretty exciting to me. Very different from the North."

OCEAN PARK NUMBER 19, 1968.

OCEAN PARK NUMBER 31, 1970–72.

DIEBENKORN IN HIS OCEAN PARK STUDIO. PHOTO BY ARNOLD CHANIN.

certainly about sensuous pleasure, but quali-
fied and tightened by an acute sense of insta-
bility: a San Andreas fault runs, as it were,
through the paradise of paint. The syntax of
Diebenkorn's work is always explicit, and in its
readiness to let the first impulses of thought
leave their traces in the finished work, it makes
the viewer witness to the process of painting:
how this too obtrusive yellow is cut back, leaving its ghost along a charcoal line; how that 45-
degree cut is sharpened, then blurred, then
hidden by veils of overpainting. To scan the
surface of a big Ocean Park is to watch these
additions become a kind of transparency,
bathing the text in calm, elevated reflection."

But more than the landscape that figured
into these new paintings, Diebenkorn's large,
light-filled studio made its presence felt as
well.

"I knew I wanted to be on the west side,
and to work out here, because of the weather,
sort of the clarity," recalled Diebenkorn. "I

"—being with
other artists...
and just sort
of catching
something of
their lives and
something of the
life of Los Angeles,
which seemed,
surprisingly,
quite attractive."

didn't realize that it had a very special kind of light. I discovered later. . . ."

After a little searching, he found the perfect west side studio:

"There were two large spaces and one small one, and a sailmaker had the front, large space. . . . There were windows to the east, large windows, transom windows. They're on a pivot and they open them, you pull them out, and they go to a sharp angle. They're cut out of a larger window, which is fixed. So there's this center with the open window, which was to my right, and right back of my painting table. Then there was this large, lighted rectangle, more of a square within it, and then, seen from the side, the transom provided the diagonal. There's just so many of the elements there, and I remember several more astute people who visited the studio said, 'Well, look, you're painting your transom windows.'"

Well, not exactly. But the studio and its view

"I remember several more astute people who visited the studio said, 'Well, look, you're painting your transom windows.'"

provided enormous inspiration. The expanses of white, the hazy rectangles of color, the sharply angled roofs in the distance, *and* the transom windows—all made their way into the *Ocean Park* series. Critic Kenneth Baker notes that "we can imagine how old Santa Monica's geometry of white-and-pastel stucco buildings punctuated by windows and sloping rooflines might underlie the pictures' architecture of lines and erasures."

Richard Diebenkorn died in 1993. His *Ocean Park* series is now recognized as a masterpiece: a bleached, angular tribute to a special place and a brilliant "landscape painter."

"I didn't realize that it had a very special kind of light. I discovered later...."

the east bay

TERRY MCMILLAN

DIABLO MAGAZINE once wrote that "Terry McMillan lives in a perfect-looking house with a perfectly kept lawn on a perfect cul-de-sac in a perfect neighborhood off Old Blackhawk Road in Danville, California." Hers is a life with all the markings of a happy, successful career.

With a string of best-selling books, including *How Stella Got Her Groove Back*, *Waiting to Exhale*, and her latest, *A Day Late and a Dollar Short*, McMillan has enjoyed tremendous success, but unlike many other artists who speak poetically of inspiration and creativity, McMillan tends to forego such expressions

MCMILLAN AT HOME IN DANVILLE. PHOTO BY MELISSA BARNES.

Instead she seems more comfortable candidly discussing her hobbies and her family's domestic shortcomings.

"Certain things drive me crazy. Like, why can't my son pick his clothes up from the floor? Or why does he have to leave food in his room for days at a time? My husband's driving is terrible. He drives like a Jamaican [which he is]. He tailgates. Last week, he hit somebody. It was like his fifth accident in five years. But when it comes to my husband, everybody says, you've got to give him credit because anyone who can tolerate your ass deserves that much."

This anchor of everyday realism carries over perfectly into McMillan's fictional world. In fact, it's this grounded attitude that brings McMillan closer to her readers. Like a lot of novelists McMillan agrees that much of the best material comes from real-life experiences.

As she told *Diablo* magazine: "I always put myself in my books. It's an opportunity

"Life throws a whole lot at you. I'm interested in discovering how my characters get through it."

for me to recognize my own weaknesses and flaws. And acknowledge them. And when I acknowledge them, I get past it."

On the subject of home, she says she originally picked Danville to settle because, "it was great for my son when he was a kid. See these hills, he's ridden his moped and his go-ped and whatever up there. He's had his boots in the creeks here. He's caught polliwogs. That's why I moved here. I wanted my son in a neighborhood where there were other little kids, where he could go outside without my worrying if he's going to get shot."

In her inimitable fashion, McMillan has a somewhat more honest approach to her home and creative environment than many other artists.

She has plans to move to Oakland in the near future and, while she loves the East Bay, about Danville now she bluntly says: "It's boring. It was boring when my son was little. I'm just waiting on a phone call. Any time now I

"I always put myself in my books. It's an opportunity for me to recognize my own weaknesses and flaws."

THE WRITER OUTSIDE HER HOME. PHOTO BY MELISSA BARNES.

want to sell this house. We're finished with this neighborhood. But the bottom line is his needs were more important than mine. And they still are. He goes to school in Berkeley now, and I don't want him driving twenty-five miles a day to school.

"But these things just kind of happen, don't they? Don't you just fall into it? Why are you here and not somewhere else? That's what happens. I could have been in L.A."

McMillan has been working on her new book and says it's "basically about a woman who says yes when she means no—and that's in life, not sex. I think about that a lot, how many women, especially in a neighborhood like this one, live this Donna Reed kind of lifestyle—everything is so perfect—how many of them live like that. I know a lot of women who are living a lie. Their whole lives revolve around their husband and kids, and there's nothing left for them. This story deals with everything that happens between that

"People come up and say, 'Hey, you look just like Terry McMillan.' And I say, 'Well, I get that a lot and I resent it. She's much older than I am.'"

"I know a lot of women who are living a lie."

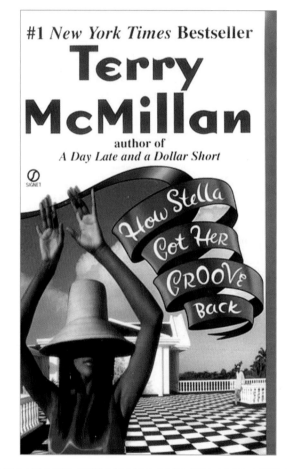

#1 *New York Times* **Bestseller**

Terry McMillan

author of
A Day Late and a Dollar Short

How Stella Got Her Groove Back

MCMILLAN'S 1997 BEST-SELLING BOOK WAS ALSO A HIT FILM.

moment and when she eventually gets in bed, puts her arms around her husband, says good morning, and she's got no hair. It's a story about women who say yes when they mean no. And how your life evolves when you do that."

While McMillan writes steadily, she isn't one to force it if the muse isn't responding. When she's not writing she likes to practice her many hobbies.

"I sew. In the wintertime I ski. I work out but I don't think of working out as a hobby. And I like to cook. Not long ago, I looked at myself and I said, you know, I used to have a hobby. And now I don't. I'm going to start to sew. You'd be surprised at how many people today don't have hobbies. These Silicon Valley people, their hobby is driving on the freeway."

"You'd be surprised at how many people today don't have hobbies. These Silicon Valley people, their hobby is driving on the freeway."

jackson

EUDORA WELTY

WHEN YOU THINK of Eudora Welty, you think of Jackson, Mississippi. The grande dame of American letters, author of thirteen books, and winner of almost every literary award in existence, spent her entire life in one town.

Not just in one town, *in one house.*

Eudora Alice Welty was born April 13, 1909, on North Congress Street in Jackson, in the house her father built with his own hands. In her autobiography, *One Writer's Beginnings,* she vividly recalls the childhood home:

"In our house, on North Congress Street in Jackson, Mississippi, where I was born, the

EUDORA WELTY'S CHILDHOOD HOME, JACKSON, MISSISSIPPI. PHOTO BY JOHN B. PADGETT.

EUDORA WELTY AT EIGHTY-THREE. PHOTO BY PHILLIP GOULD.

oldest of three children, in 1909, we grew up to the striking of clocks. There was a mission-style oak grandfather clock standing in the hall, which sent its gonglike strokes through the living room, dining room, kitchen, and pantry, and up the sounding board of the stairwell. Through the night, it could find its way into our ears; sometimes, even on the sleeping porch, midnight could wake us up.

"My parents' bedroom had a smaller striking clock that answered it. Though the kitchen clock did nothing but show the time, the dining room clock was a cuckoo clock with weights on long chains, one of which my baby brother, after climbing on a chair to the top of the china closet, once succeeded in suspending the cat from for a moment.

"I don't know whether or not my father's family, in having been Swiss back in the 1700s before the first three Welty brothers came to America, had anything to do with this; but we all of us have been time-minded all our lives.

"It is through place that we put out roots . . . but where those roots reach toward . . . is the deep and running vein, eternal and consistent and everywhere purely itself. . . ."

This was good, at least for a future fiction writer, being able to learn so penetratingly, and almost first of all, about chronology. It was one of the good many things I learned almost without knowing it; it would be there when I needed it."

Welty did leave Jackson—and her family— to attend college. She began at Mississippi State and two years later transferred to the University of Wisconsin at Madison. But after she graduated, the Great Depression hit, and she returned home. That same year, her father suddenly died. Welty remained.

That was when she began to write. Her first stories chronicled her bus travels across rural Mississippi for the Works Progress Administration in the 1930s.

"I went all over Mississippi," she recalled. "This was the most important thing to me, because I'd never seen it. The experience was the real germ of my wanting to become a real writer, a true writer."

"One can only say: writers must always write best of what they know, and sometimes they do it by staying where they know it."

From that moment, she was hooked. And from that moment, the landscape of Mississippi would infuse her writing. Welty was a writer who placed much importance on where she lived:

"It is by the nature of itself that fiction is all bound up in the local. The internal reason for that is surely that feelings are bound up in place. The human mind is a mass of associations—associations more poetic even than actual. . . . Surely place induces poetry."

Welty's books *Losing Battles, A Curtain of Green, The Robber Bridegroom,* and *The Eye of the Story* gained her international fame and a Pulitzer Prize. But she remained in Jackson, on North Congress Street.

Her friend the writer Willie Morris describes the house that was such a bedrock for Welty and her writing:

The nearby streets were gravel and there were whispery pine forests all around. On the front lawn is a majestic oak tree. ('Never cut

"I went all over Mississippi. . . . I'd never seen it. [This] was the real germ of my wanting to become a real writer, a true writer."

an oak,' her mother advised her.) The kitchen of the old house looks out on a deep-green garden with its formal bench beneath another towering oak tree. Eudora loved what she called 'my mother's garden' and says she was 'my mother's yard boy.'

"Her Tudor-style house has a sturdy vestibule, a brown gabled roof on the second story, and a screened-in side porch long unused.

"Excluding the time she spent traveling, she lived and worked there over seventy-five years. 'I like being in the house where nobody else has ever lived but my own family,' she said, 'even though it's lonely being the only person left.'

"She called it 'my unruly home.' Books of all kinds were everywhere, stacked in corners, on tables and chairs. There were mountains of books, and on every flat surface one found unanswered mail. Her correspondence was so voluminous, she said, that she was unable to handle it. In a box on the table was the Richard Wright Medal of Literary

"Surely place induces poetry."

EUDORA WELTY

One Writer's Beginnings

Excellence she received in 1994. 'I'm proud to have it,' she said."

Eudora Welty never married. Until her death in 2001, she lived on North Congress Street. Today, the home is a bustling office space; camellias drape the porches. A plaque in the front yard notes that many of the events depicted in *One Writer's Beginnings* took place in this house.

Some writers have landscapes; Eudora Welty had a house. In her *Collected Essays,* Eudora Welty explained why place mattered so much to her writing:

"It is through place that we put out roots, wherever birth, chance, fate, or our traveling selves set us down; but where those roots reach toward—whether in America, England, or Timbuktu—is the deep and running vein, eternal and consistent and everywhere purely itself, that feeds and is fed by the human understanding."

Maybe the best example of how her sur-

"I like being in the house where nobody else has ever lived but my own family, even though it's lonely being the only person left."

roundings influenced her work comes from Willie Morris:

"Directly across the street from the Welty home was the music building of Belhaven College, and from the practice rooms the sound of piano music would drift across Pinehurst Street, keeping her company through the long and solitary hours at the old Royal. 'Though I was as constant in my work as the students were,' she has written, 'subconsciously I must have been listening to them, following them. . . . I realized that each practice session reached to me as an outpouring. And those longings, so expressed, so insistent, called up my longings unexpressed. I began to hear, in what kept coming from across the street into the room where I typed, the recurring dreams of youth, inescapable, never to be renounced, naming themselves over and over again.'"

"I began to hear, in what kept coming from across the street into the room where I typed, the recurring dreams of youth. . . ."

big sur

HENRY MILLER

THREE HOURS SOUTH OF San Francisco, Highway 1 careens to the coast and is swallowed in an enormous redwood grove. Shrouded in thick fog, on the sheer mountain side of the highway, sits the Henry Miller Library.

Henry Valentine Miller was born a continent away, in New York City, in 1891. As a youth, he dreamed of being a writer and did what it took to become one, including selling poems door-to-door and managing a Greenwich Village speakeasy. In 1930, on a trip to Paris he met the writer Anaïs Nin, who helped him publish the work that would

HENRY AND EVE MILLER, BIG SUR. PHOTO BY WINN BULLOCK.

make him famous. *Tropic of Cancer* was an autobiographical novel about expatriate life in Paris so sexually explicit that it was banned in all English-speaking countries.

In February 1944, the embattled author made a trip to the wild coastal lands of Big Sur —now the home of the Esalen Institute and a mecca over the years for free-spirited writers, artists, and hippies.

Miller arrived in the midst of a torrential downpour, but immediately felt at home. He felt, somehow, that he had found the real California. As he put it: "This is the California that men dreamed of years ago, this is the Pacific that Balboa looked out on from the Peak of Darien, this is the face of the earth as the Creator intended it to look."

The writer was mesmerized with Big Sur's rugged, isolated coastline. "Here I will find peace," he wrote in his journals. "Here I shall find the strength to do the work I was made to do."

" . . . this is the face of the earth as the Creator intended it to look."

And he did. Henry Miller's new home contributed to some of the most important writing of his career, including *The Rosy Crucifixion,* a three-volume epic; and the classic *Big Sur and the Oranges of Hieronymus Bosch,* the story of his life on the coast.

Once he settled in California, Miller's fortunes changed. His new works began impressing the literary establishment, and when a legal decision held that *Tropic of Cancer* was not obscene, his older works began being republished. In addition, the now noted author also began to receive recognition as a water colorist.

Miller's newfound royalties enabled him to live comfortably in Big Sur, even allowing him to purchase a modest house on Partington Ridge. In *Big Sur and the Oranges of Hieronymus Bosch,* he remembers back: "I like to think back on my early days on Partington Ridge, when there was no electricity, no butane tanks, no refrigeration—and the mail

"Here the redwood made its last stand. At dawn its majesty is almost painful to behold."

THE VIEW FROM MILLER'S HOME. PHOTO BY MAGNUS TORÉN.

HENRY MILLER AND HIS FOURTH WIFE, EVE, AT HOME IN BIG SUR. PHOTO BY WINN BULLOCK.

came only three times a week. In those days, and even when I returned to the Ridge, I managed to get along without a car. . . ."

Here on the Partington Ridge, with his third wife, Lepska, he raised his two children, Valentine and Tony. Each day, Miller became more entranced with the raw nature surrounding him: "There are two magic hours of the day which I have only really come to know and wait for, bathe in, I might say, since living here. One is dawn, the other sunset. In both we have what I like to think of as 'the true light': the one cold, the other warm, but both creating an ambiance of super-reality, or the reality behind reality. . . . Everything is brush and cones, umbrellas of light—the leaves, boughs, stalks, trunks standing out separate and defined, as if etched by the Creator himself."

At first, the writer thought Big Sur "the ideal place in which to work." But, over the years, he discovered something even deeper, more profound: "I enjoy working when I

"Peace and solitude! I have had a taste of it, even here in America."

can...[but] whether I work or whether I don't has come to assume less and less importance. I have had here some of the most bitter experiences of my life; I have also known here some of the most exalted moments. Sweet or bitter, I am now convinced that all experience is enriching and rewarding. Above all, instructive."

Henry Miller came to Big Sur looking for a place to write. What he found was a small community of artists and a vast landscape that changed his life. On this foggy coast, the cynical author melted away, and Henry Miller rediscovered the things that matter. As he wrote in *Big Sur and the Oranges of Hieronymus Bosch:*

"This place can be a paradise . . . the *only* paradise, after all.

Peace and solitude! I have had a taste of it, even here in America. Ah, those first days on Partington Ridge! On rising I would go to the cabin door and, casting my eyes over the velvety,

"[It has] that same prehistoric look. The look of always. Nature smiling at herself in the mirror of eternity."

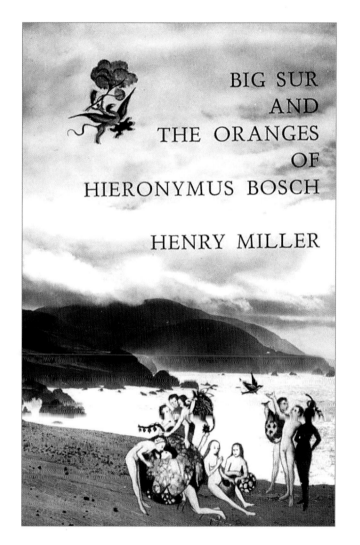

BIG SUR
AND
THE ORANGES
OF
HIERONYMUS BOSCH

HENRY MILLER

"It is a
region where
extremes meet, a
region where
one is always
conscious of
weather,
of space, of
grandeur, and
of eloquent
silence."

rolling hills, such a feeling of contentment, such a feeling of gratitude was mine that instinctively my hand went up in benediction. Blessings! Blessings on you, one and all! I blessed the trees, the birds, the dogs, the cats, I blessed the flowers, the pomegranates, the thorny cactus, I blessed men and women everywhere, no matter on what side of the fence they happened to be.

"That is how I like to begin each day. A day well begun, I say. And that is why I choose to remain here, on the slopes of the Santa Lucia, where to give thanks to the Creator comes natural and easy. Out yonder, they may curse, revile, and torture one another, defile all the human instincts, make a shambles of creation (if it were in their power), but here, no, here it is unthinkable, here there is abiding peace, the peace of God, and the serene security created by a handful of good neighbors living at one with the creature world, with noble, ancient trees, scrub

"I am just having a good time. I think this is a very important part of life—that people learn how to play, and that they make life a game, rather than a struggle for goals."

and sagebrush, wild lilac and lovely lupin, with poppies and buzzards, eagles and humming birds, gophers and rattlesnakes, and sea and sky unending."

Henry Miller lived in Big Sur until 1962, when he retired to Pacific Palisades, where he resided until his death in 1980.

After his death, lifelong friend Emil White decided to maintain his property as a memorial and as a gallery where local artists could show their work. It continues today, amid the ancient redwoods, as the Henry Miller Library, a public benefit, nonprofit organization championing the literary, artistic, and cultural contributions of the late writer, artist, and very content Big Sur resident.

"... Such a feeling of gratitude was mine that instinctively my hand went up in benediction.... Blessings on you, one and all!"

walden pond

HENRY DAVID THOREAU

AT A CERTAIN SEASON of our life
we are accustomed to consider every spot as
the possible site of a house. I have thus sur-
veyed the country on every side within a
dozen miles of where I live. . . .

What is a house but a *sedes*, a seat?—better
if a country seat. I discovered many a site for
a house not likely to be soon improved, which
some might have thought too far from the village, but to my eyes the village was too far
from it. Well, there I might live, I said; and
there I did live, for an hour, a summer and a
winter life; saw how I could let the years run
off, buffet the winter through, and see the

THOREAU CABIN, WALDEN POND.

WALDEN;

OR,

LIFE IN THE WOODS.

By HENRY D. THOREAU,

AUTHOR OF "A WEEK ON THE CONCORD AND MERRIMACK RIVERS."

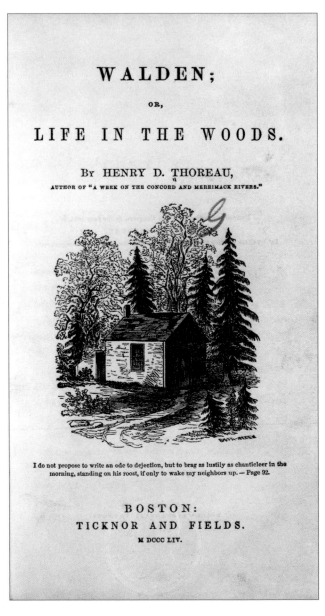

I do not propose to write an ode to dejection, but to brag as lustily as chanticleer in the morning, standing on his roost, if only to wake my neighbors up. — Page 92.

BOSTON:

TICKNOR AND FIELDS.

M DCCC LIV.

A REPRINT OF THE FIRST EDITION COVER OF *WALDEN*.

spring come in. The future inhabitants of this region, wherever they may place their houses, may be sure that they have been anticipated. An afternoon sufficed to lay out the land into orchard, wood-lot, and pasture, and to decide what fine oaks or pines should be left to stand before the door, and whence each blasted tree could be seen to the best advantage; and then I let it lie, fallow perchance, for a man is rich in proportion to the number of things which he can afford to let alone. . . .

When first I took up my abode in the woods, that is, began to spend my nights as well as days there, which, by accident, was on Independence Day, or the Fourth of July, 1845, my house was not finished for winter, but was merely a defense against the rain, without plastering or chimney, the walls being of rough, weather-stained boards, with wide chinks, which made it cool at night. The upright white hewn studs and freshly planed door and window casings give it a clean and

"I am monarch of all I *survey*, my right there is none to dispute."

airy look, especially in the morning, when its timbers were saturated with dew, so that I fancied that by noon some sweet gum would exude from them. To my imagination it retained throughout the day more or less of this auroral character, reminding me of a certain house on a mountain which I had visited a year before. This was an airy and unplastered cabin, fit to entertain a travelling god, and where a goddess might trail her garments. The winds which passed over my dwelling were such as sweep over the ridges of mountains, bearing the broken strains, or celestial parts only, of terrestrial music. The morning wind forever blows, the poem of creation is uninterrupted; but few are the ears that hear it. Olympus is but the outside of the earth everywhere. . . .

I was seated by the shore of a small pond, about a mile and a half south of the village of Concord and somewhat higher than it, in the midst of an extensive wood between that town

"This was an airy and unplastered cabin, fit to entertain a travelling god, and where a goddess might trail her garments."

and Lincoln.... whenever I looked out on the pond it impressed me like a tarn high up on the side of a mountain, its bottom far above the surface of other lakes, and, as the sun arose, I saw it throwing off its nightly clothing of mist, and here and there, by degrees, its soft ripples or its smooth reflecting surface was revealed, while the mists, like ghosts, were stealthily withdrawing in every direction into the woods, as at the breaking up of some nocturnal conventicle. The very dew seemed to hang upon the trees later into the day than usual, as on the sides of mountains.

This small lake was of most value as a neighbor in the intervals of a gentle rainstorm in August, when, both air and water being perfectly still, but the sky overcast, mid-afternoon had all the serenity of evening, and the wood thrush sang around, and was heard from shore to shore.

I went to the woods because I wished to live deliberately, to front only the essential

"The mass of men lead lives of quiet desperation.... But it is a characteristic of wisdom not to do desperate things."

A PANORAMIC VIEW OF WALDEN POND.

"I never
found the
companion
that was so
companion-
able as
solitude."

facts of life, and see if I could not learn what
it had to teach, and not, when I came to die,
discover that I had not lived. I did not wish to
live what was not life, living is so dear; nor
did I wish to practice resignation, unless it
was quite necessary. I wanted to live deep
and suck out all the marrow of life, to live
so sturdily and Spartan-like as to put to rout
all that was not life, to cut a broad swath
and shave close, to drive life into a corner,
and reduce it to its lowest terms, and, if it
proved to be mean, why then to get the whole
and genuine meanness of it, and publish its
meanness to the world; or if it were sublime,
to know it by experience, and be able to give
a true account of it in my next excursion. For
most men, it appears to me, are in a strange
uncertainty about it, whether it is of the devil
or of God, and have *somewhat hastily* con-
cluded that it is the chief end of man here to
"glorify God and enjoy him forever."

Still, we live meanly, like ants; though the

fable tells us that we were long ago changed into men; like pygmies we fight with cranes; it is error upon error, and clout upon clout, and our best virtue has for its occasion a superfluous and evitable wretchedness. Our life is frittered away by detail. An honest man has hardly need to count more than his ten fingers, or in extreme cases he may add his ten toes, and lump the rest. Simplicity, simplicity, simplicity! I say, let your affairs be as two or three, and not a hundred or a thousand; instead of a million count half a dozen, and keep your accounts on your thumb-nail. In the midst of this chopping sea of civilized life, such are the clouds and storms and quicksands and thousand-and-one items to be allowed for, that a man has to live, if he would not founder and go to the bottom and not make his port at all, by dead reckoning, and he must be a great calculator indeed who succeeds. Simplify, simplify.

"We must learn to re-awaken and keep ourselves awake, not by mechanical aids, but by an infinite expectation of the dawn...."

acknowledgments

Cover image "Porch dusk" © 1989 by Joel
Meyerowitz. Reprinted by permission of the
photographer.

Introduction © 2002 by John Miller and Aaron Kenedi.

Peter Matthiessen images: "Peter Matthiessen in His
Studio" © by Arnold Newman. Reprinted by permission of GettyOne Images. "Whale" and "Long Island
Fishermen" © by Doug Kuntz. Reprinted by permission of Doug Kuntz.

O'Keeffe letters: "To Anita Pollitzer, 1916," "To Anita
Pollitzer, 1948," "To William Schubart, 1950," "To
William Schubart, 1950" reprinted by permission of
the Georgia O'Keeffe Foundation.

Georgia O'Keeffe images: "Georgia O'Keeffe in Juan
Hamilton's Studio," "O'Keeffe's Studio in Abiquiu,
NM," "Georgia O'Keeffe Pouring Tea" and "Ladder
and Adobe Wall," all © by Todd Webb. Reprinted by
permission of the Evans Gallery. *Wall with Green Door*
by Georgia O'Keeffe, © 1952 The Corcoran Gallery of
Art/Corbis. Reprinted by permission of Corbis Photo
Archive.

Larry McMurtry excerpt by Mark Horowitz, © 1997
by Mark Horowitz. Originally appeared in *The New
York Times Magazine*, November 1997. Reprinted by
permission of the author.

McMurtry portrait © 1997 by Michael O'Brien.
Reprinted by permission of the photographer.

"Cotton and Replanted Grassland on the Texas High Plains" © 1997 by Tom Bean/Corbis. Reprinted by permission of Corbis Photo Archive.

Anne Rice excerpt by Susan Ferraro. Originally appeared in *The New York Times Magazine*, October 14, 1990. Reprinted by permission of The New York Times Agency.

Anne Rice images: "Rice with Family" and "Artist's Portrait" © by Rick Olivier. Reprinted by permission of the photographer. "St. Louis Cathedral, New Orleans" © by Mike Brinson. Reprinted by permission of GettyOne Images.

Gary Snyder images: "Snyder in the Foothills," "The Artist's Studio," and "The Family Compound" all © by Ed Kashi. Reprinted by permission of Ed Kashi.

Diebenkorn excerpts from interview with Susan Larsen © 1985 The Smithsonian Institution. Reprinted courtesy The Smithsonian Institution.

Richard Diebenkorn images: "Empty Beach, Santa Monica" © by Ryan McVay. Reprinted by permission of GettyOne Images. *Ocean Park number 19* © 1968 by Richard Diebenkorn. Reprinted by permission of the San Francisco Museum of Modern Art. *Ocean Park number 31* © 1970–72 by Christies Images/Corbis. Reprinted by permission of Corbis Photo Archive. "Portrait of Richard Diebenkorn © 1985 by Arnold Chanin. Reprinted by permission of the Smithsonian Institution.

McMillan images: "The Artist in Her Living Room" and "The Artist outside Her Home" both © by Melissa Barnes. Reprinted by permission of Melissa Barnes.

Eudora Welty images: "Childhood Home" © 1997 by John B. Padgett. Reprinted by permission of the photographer. Welty portrait by Phillip Gould © 1992 by Phillip Gould/Corbis. Reprinted by permission of Corbis Photo Archive.

Excerpts from *Big Sur and the Oranges of Hieronymus Bosch* by Henry Miller, © 1978 by Henry Miller. Reprinted by permission of W.W. Norton & Company.

Henry Miller images: "Henry and Eve on the Road" and "Henry and Eve Miller" © by Winn Bullock. Reprinted by permission of Barbara and Gene Bullock-Wilson. "Big Sur Coastline" © 2002 by Magnus Torén. Reprinted by permission of the photographer.

Henry David Thoreau images: "The Cabin at Walden Pond," "First Edition of Walden," and "Walden Pond Scenic," © Corbis Photo Archive. Reprinted by permission of Corbis Photo Archive.